Faith to Elevate – 30 Day Devotional
Copyright © 2025 by Slavoski L. Wright Sr.
All rights reserved. No part of this book may be reproduced, stored in a retrieval system, or transmitted in any form or by any means, electronic, mechanical, photocopying, recording, or otherwise, without prior written permission from the publisher, except for brief quotations used in reviews or scholarly works.

Unless otherwise indicated, all Scripture quotations are taken from the Holy Bible, New International Version®, NIV®. Copyright ©1973, 1978, 1984, 2011 by Biblica, Inc.™ Used by permission. All rights reserved worldwide.

This book is a work of faith-based inspiration. It is not intended as a substitute for professional counseling or medical advice. The author and publisher disclaim any liability from the use or misuse of the content herein.

ISBN: 979-8-218-73081-9
Publisher: Making It Wright Counseling & Consulting PLLC (MIWCC).

Printed in the United States of America.

Dedication

To every believer no matter where you are in your faith journey.

Whether you are new to the faith, struggling to hold on, growing stronger, or already walking in **great boldness** this is for you.

This devotional is dedicated to you as a reminder that:

God sees you.
God is with you.
And God is still calling you **higher**.

Every step counts. Every prayer matters. And your faith right where it is, is the foundation for elevation.

So keep going.
Keep trusting.
And never stop believing that **faith still works**.

With love and expectation,
Dr. Slavoski L. Wright Sr.

~ Faith ~

lifts you <u>higher</u> than fear ever could hold you down.

About the Author

Dr. Slavoski L. Wright Sr. is a passionate pastor, faith-builder, and dynamic leader who has faithfully served in ministry for over two decades. With a heart for preaching, mentoring, and helping others discover their purpose, he is known for his authentic voice, spiritual depth, and unwavering commitment to developing strong, faith-filled believers.

Dr. Wright currently serves as the Senior Pastor of Greater El Bethel – Dallas, a historic church located in the heart of the Tenth Street Freedman's Town of Dallas, Texas. He brings vision and vitality to this sacred space, blending biblical conviction with community compassion to lead a multigenerational congregation into a season of restoration and impact.

Alongside his pastoral calling, Dr. Wright has served over 16 years in law enforcement and currently holds the position of Police Lieutenant within a leading healthcare system, overseeing operations across multiple hospital campuses. His leadership in both sacred and secular arenas reflects his belief that faith and service are not separate but intertwined.

He holds a Doctor of Divinity from North Central Theological Seminary, and both a Master's and Bachelor's degree in Christian Ministry from Wayland Baptist University. He is a certified Master Peace Officer, Field Training Officer, and instructor well respected for his commitment to excellence and integrity in every role.

Dr. Wright is the co-author along with his wife of *Blended and Loving It: Thirty-Day Devotional for Blended Families*. He is also deeply passionate about cultivating strong faith in others in which God led him to write this *Faith to Elevate Thirty Day Devotional*. His life's message is simple yet powerful: *you were created to rise, and faith is the fuel that gets you there.*

He is a devoted husband to Umeka Wright, a loving father of six children, and a proud grandfather. Above all, he is a servant of God, committed to inspiring others to live boldly, love deeply, and walk by faith every step of the way.

Connect with Dr. Wright:
 pastor@gebdallas.org
 www.gebdallas.org

Congratulations!!! You've taken the first step. Regardless of where you are, you still have what it takes to ELEVATE your life!

Table of Contents

Find Your Place. Follow Your Journey. Keep Elevating.

Table of Contents

Preface
Introduction

Week 1: Foundation of Elevating Faith

Day 1 – Faith Is the Foundation
Day 2 – Faith Comes Alive Through the Word
Day 3 – Speak to It in Faith
Day 4 – Live By It, Not Just Talk About It
Day 5 – Faith Over Feelings
Day 6 – Faith Without Action Is Dead
Day 7 – Trust the Process

Week 2: Faith That Obeys God

Day 8 – Obedience Unlocks Elevation
Day 9 – Love Is Proven by Obedience
Day 10 – Obedience in the Ordinary
Day 11 – Don't Just Hear It…. Do It
Day 12 – Obedience Is Better Than Sacrifice
Day 13 – Why Call Him Lord, But Don't Obey?
Day 14 – Obedience That Leads to Glory

Week 3: Faith That Conquers Fear

Day 15 – Fear Not, God Is With You
Day 16 – Fear Is Not from God
Day 17 – When I Am Afraid, I Will Trust
Day 18 – Faith Walks on What Fear Drowns In
Day 19 – Be Strong and Courageous
Day 20 – Delivered From All My Fears
Day 21 – Why Are You Afraid? Where Is Your Faith?

Week 4: Faith to Endure and Overcome

Day 22 – Count It All Joy
Day 23 – Pressure Produces Perseverance
Day 24 – Don't Grow Weary
Day 25 – Wait On the Lord
Day 26 – Pressed But Not Crushed
Day 27 – Your Faith Is More Precious Than Gold
Day 28 – Hold Fast to Your Confession

Week 5: Faith to Elevate Others

Day 29 – Let Your Light Shine
Day 30 – Run Your Race With Bold Faith

Preface

There comes a time in every believer's life when faith can no longer be casual, it must be *Elevated*. Faith must rise above fear, above comfort, and above what is seen in order to fully embrace what God has spoken. This 30-day journey was birthed out of that truth.

Faith to Elevate! is more than a devotional, it is a call to action. It is for the person who believes God has more for their life but needs the courage to move forward. It is for the weary soul who needs fresh strength, the faithful heart that has been tested by trials, and the leader who is tired of pouring from an empty place.

Each entry was prayerfully written to meet you right where you are, speak life into your day, and point you toward the next level of your walk with God. My hope is that over these 30 days, your faith won't just be encouraged, it will be *Activated*.

Let's grow. Let's trust again. Let's elevate.

~ Dr. Slavoski L. Wright Sr.
Pastor, Servant, and Believer in Bigger

Introduction

You don't need more time, you need more *faith*.
The kind that believes in spite of, walks through storms, and obeys when it is inconvenient.
The kind that shifts your perspective, transforms your mindset, and aligns your steps with God's purpose.

This devotional is designed to walk with you for 30 days as you build a faith that does not just survive, but *soars*. Each day includes:

- A powerful **Scripture** to anchor your thoughts
- A short **Devotional Thought** with real world application
- A **Reflection** prompt to help you dig deeper
- A **Prayer** to keep your spirit focused
- A **Declaration For The Day** to speak faith over your life

Whether you are reading this at sunrise, over lunch, or just before bed, know that these moments matter. God is drawing you closer, stretching your trust, and preparing you for elevation.

You were never meant to stay stuck.
You were created to climb.
Welcome to the journey of *Faith to Elevate!*

Begin with a positive mind, and a positive intent.

Before You Begin:
My Faith to Elevate Reflection

Before you start this 30-day journey, take a moment to pause, breathe, and set your heart in expectation. This space is for you to write down what you are believing God for, what you are hoping to learn, and how you desire to grow over the next 30 days.

This devotional is not just words on a page, it is a partnership between you, your faith, and your future. So be honest with yourself. Dream boldly. Write it down and come back to it when the days get hard.

May these pages remind you that you are not starting alone, you are starting with faith that will elevate you.

What am I hoping to gain from this devotional?

_____

_____

_____

_____

_____

_____

_____

_____

_____

_____

My prayer for this journey:

HERE WE GO.........
LET'S ELEVATE!!!

***

WEEK 1:
~ FOUNDATION OF ELEVATING FAITH~

Build strong. Stand firm. Grow deeper.

***

Day 1

~ Faith Is the Foundation ~

📖 Scripture Focus:
"Now faith is the substance of things hoped for, the evidence of things not seen."
~ Hebrews 11:1 (KJV)

📄 Devotional Thought

If you're going to elevate, you have to believe first. Faith is not a spiritual luxury, it is a *necessity*. It is the solid ground beneath every spiritual step forward. When everything around you says, "not yet," faith says "right now." When life says, "you can't," faith whispers, "with God, I already have."

This verse is not just poetic, it is power-packed. It reminds us that faith is substance (something real) and **evidence** (something reliable). Even when your circumstances show no sign of change, your faith testifies that breakthrough is still coming. It is the confident assurance that what God promised will come to pass, even when you can't trace Him, you still trust Him.

Faith isn't just believing in God, it is believing **God.** There's a difference. The first says "He exists." The second says, "I'll obey, I'll move, and I'll trust, because He said it."

You don't need to know how God will do it. You just need to believe that He will. Faith to Elevate says, God is my foundation.

Reflection Thought

What area of your life needs a fresh foundation of faith? Is it your family, finances, career, or your calling? Today, take one bold step of faith in that area and pray over it, plan for it, or prepare as if it is already done.

_____

_____

_____

_____

_____

_____

_____

_____

Prayer of Elevation

Father, today I choose to believe You beyond what I see. Help me stand on faith, not fear. On Your Word, not my worry. Lay a new foundation in me that causes me to rise above doubt and move toward destiny. Elevate my trust, expand my vision, and ground me in unshakable faith. In Jesus' name, Amen.

Declaration For The Day

"My faith is my foundation, and with it, I'm rising higher today!"

Day 2

~ Faith Comes Alive Through the Word ~

📖 Scripture Focus

"So then faith cometh by hearing, and hearing by the word of God."
~ Romans 10:17 (KJV)

✍ Devotional Thought

If you want elevated faith, you have to feed it. Faith isn't born from thin air, it is born from the Word. Just like our bodies need food to grow, our spirits need God's truth to thrive. Faith comes *by hearing*, not just once, but continually, consistently, and intentionally.

It is not just about hearing a preacher or reading a verse, it is about *receiving* what God is saying and letting it rewire your belief system. Every time you open the Bible, faith is being stirred. Every time you hear God's promises spoken over your life, your spiritual muscles flex a little more.

The problem isn't always a lack of faith, it is a lack of Word intake. You can't run a marathon on an empty tank, and you can't walk by faith if you're starving spiritually. God's Word builds your perspective, fuels your prayers, and equips your obedience.

You don't just need motivation, you need *revelation*. And that comes when you put yourself in position to hear from God daily.

🌀 Reflection Thought

When was the last time you truly listened for God's voice through His Word? Choose one verse today to meditate on throughout your day. Write it down, speak it aloud, or set it as your phone background. Let it feed your faith.

_____
_____
_____
_____
_____
_____
_____
_____

🙏 Prayer of Elevation

Lord, open my ears and my heart to hear Your Word clearly. Feed me with truth that strengthens, corrects, and inspires me. I don't want weak faith. I want *elevated* faith that grows every day. Draw me into Your Word like never before. In Jesus' name, Amen.

📣 Declaration For The Day

"God's Word is fueling my faith. I'm hearing, believing, and rising higher!"

Day 3

~ Speak to It in Faith ~

📖 Scripture Focus
"For verily I say unto you, That whosoever shall say unto this mountain, Be thou removed, and be thou cast into the sea... he shall have whatsoever he saith."
~ Mark 11:23 (KJV)

✍ Devotional Thought

Faith isn't just something you feel, it is something you **say.** Jesus made it clear: your words carry the authority to move mountains. But here's the key, He didn't say, "Think about the mountain," or "Complain about the mountain." He said, *"Speak to it."*

Elevated faith does not stay silent. It opens its mouth and speaks life, breakthrough, and victory even while the mountain is still standing in the way. If you're going to rise, your speech has to rise too. Faith-filled people talk differently. They declare the promise before they see the performance.

Many people have mountain-sized problems and pebble-sized faith because they've been *rehearsing* their issues instead of *releasing* their faith. Releasing your faith means trusting God enough to speak and act like His Word is already true, even before you see the outcome. Stop empowering the obstacle. Start activating your elevation by speaking what God said. Not what fear, doubt, or negativity says.

Don't wait for things to change before you speak up. Speak up and watch things begin to change.

Reflection Thought:

What's the "mountain" in your life that needs a faith-filled word spoken to it? Take 60 seconds today and *literally speak out loud* what you're believing God to do. Speak the Word over your situation boldly and without apology.

_____
_____
_____
_____
_____
_____
_____
_____

Prayer of Elevation:

God, I thank You for giving me the authority to speak in faith. Help me not to speak from fear or frustration, but from truth. Let my mouth be a weapon of elevation, declaring what You've promised over what I see. I speak life, victory, healing, and breakthrough today. In Jesus' name, Amen.

Declaration For The Day:

"I speak with bold faith. Mountains move when I open my mouth!"

Day 4

~ Live By It, Not Just Talk About It ~

Scripture Focus
"...but the just shall live by his faith."
~ Habakkuk 2:4 (KJV)

Devotional Thought

Faith isn't just something you pull out in a crisis. It is a *lifestyle*. It is not reserved for Sunday mornings or spiritual highs; it is how you think, move, give, forgive, and dream *every single day*. God never intended for faith to be occasional. It is how the just are called to *live*.

To "live by faith" means your decisions reflect God's promises more than people's opinions or your own comfort. It is waking up every morning with a confidence that God is in control, even when nothing looks like it. It is choosing to believe when it is easier to quit, trust when it is tempting to worry, and obey when it is not convenient.

Real elevation comes when faith becomes your rhythm, not your reaction. When it is not just something you *talk about*, but something you *walk out*.

Living by faith means elevating and letting your faith be visible even when your victory isn't.

🗨 Reflection Thought:

How would your day look different if you lived by faith in *every* area? Identify one decision today where you can choose faith over fear, faith over feelings, or faith over familiarity, and act on it.

_____

_____

_____

_____

_____

_____

_____

_____

🙏 Prayer of Elevation

Lord, I don't want to just talk faith, I want to live it. Help me to make faith my lifestyle, not my last resort. Teach me to walk daily in confidence, courage, and obedience to You. Let my life be a living testimony that faith works. In Jesus' name, Amen.

📣 Declaration For The Day

"I don't just talk faith. I live by it, and I'm walking in elevation!"

Day 5

~ Faith Over Feelings ~

📖 Scripture Focus
"For we walk by faith, not by sight:"
~ 2 Corinthians 5:7 (KJV)

✍ Devotional Thought

Feelings are real, but they aren't always reliable. Elevating in faith means you learn to move beyond what you *feel* and respond to what you *know* God said. Sight says, "This does not make sense." Faith says, "God's plan is still in motion."

Walking by faith means trusting that God is working behind the scenes, even when you can't see a thing. It is the kind of trust that says, "I don't feel strong, but I believe I'm still victorious." It is pressing forward even when your emotions are dragging behind.

You may feel tired, but keep walking.
You may feel uncertain, but keep trusting.
You may feel overlooked, but you're still chosen.

Faith does not require a good mood to move forward. It just requires that you *believe more than you feel.* Your feelings may fluctuate, but your faith does not have to.

Reflection Thought:

What emotion is trying to hold your faith hostage today? Call it out. Then call it under submission to what God has spoken. Replace a feeling with a *faith action*. Respond to fear with a praise. Respond to doubt with a decision. Do this daily.

_____

_____

_____

_____

_____

_____

_____

_____

Prayer of Elevation

Lord, thank You that I don't have to be ruled by my emotions. When I feel unsure, remind me of what You promised. Help me walk by faith, even when I can't see the full picture. Anchor me in trust so I can move forward with boldness. In Jesus' name, Amen.

Declaration For The Day

"My feelings don't lead me, my faith does. I'm walking in divine elevation!"

Day 6

~ Faith Without Action Is Dead ~

📖 Scripture Focus
"Even so faith, if it hath not works, is dead, being alone."
~ James 2:17 (KJV)

✎ Devotional Thought

Faith isn't just belief, it is behavior. You can say you trust God all day long, but if there's no movement, no obedience, and no response, the faith you're claiming is just theory. Real faith takes action. Even when it is scary, uncomfortable, or does not make complete sense.

God honors faith that *moves*. He's not just listening for what we say, He's watching for what we'll do. Will we apply for the job? Will we forgive the person? Will we give even when it stretches us? Will we show up where He told us to go?

Faith is the bridge between what you believe and what you do. It turns "I trust God" into "Watch me follow Him." It does not wait until everything feels perfect. It says, "Let's go," even if the path isn't fully lit.

If you're believing God for elevation, ask yourself, what action am I taking to match my faith?

Reflection Thought

Is there an area in your life where you've been talking faith but not walking it out? Identify one small step you can take today that aligns your actions with your belief.

_____
_____
_____
_____
_____
_____
_____
_____

Prayer of Elevation

God, I don't want to just say I have faith. I want to live like I believe You. Help me put my faith into motion. Show me where I've been passive and give me the courage to act boldly. Let my life be evidence that faith works. In Jesus' name, Amen.

Declaration For The Day

"I put feet to my faith. Today I move, obey, and elevate!"

Day 7

~ Trust the Process ~

📖 Scripture Focus
"Trust in the Lord with all thine heart; and lean not unto thine own understanding. In all thy ways acknowledge him, and he shall direct thy paths."
~ Proverbs 3:5–6 (KJV)

✎ Devotional Thought

One of the greatest acts of faith is *trusting God when you don't understand Him.* Let's be honest, there are moments when His timing does not match your urgency, when His route feels like a detour, or when He's silent when you need answers. But trust says, "Even when I can't trace Him, I'll still follow Him."

Elevated faith chooses surrender over control. It says, "God, I don't know how, but I know You." Trust is what steadies your heart when the road gets bumpy. It is what anchors your mind when fear tries to hijack your decisions. It is what allows you to sleep at night, even when the situation isn't solved.

Stop leaning on your limited understanding. Lean into the One who holds the full picture. The path may not be clear, but the Guide is trustworthy.

Reflection Thought

Where have you been leaning on your own understanding lately? In prayer today, release it. Write it down, speak it out, and declare your full trust in God's direction, even if you don't have all the details yet.

_____

_____

_____

_____

_____

_____

_____

_____

Prayer of Elevation

Father, I release control and lean into Your wisdom. Even when I don't see the full picture, I choose to trust You with my whole heart. Direct my steps, guard my heart, and guide my path. I believe Your plan is greater than anything I could come up with on my own. In Jesus' name, Amen.

Declaration For The Day

"I trust God with all my heart. He's directing my path, and I'm walking into elevation!"

Week 1 Reflection: *Foundation of Elevating Faith*

Take a moment to reflect on how you laid a stronger foundation this week. Celebrate what you discovered about your faith and where you're trusting God to keep building you up.

What did I learn this week about building a strong foundation in my faith?

_____

_____

_____

_____

_____

What did God reveal to me about areas that need strengthening?

_____

_____

_____

_____

_____

Where do I feel more stable in my walk with Him?

_____

_____

_____

_____

_____

One thing I will continue building on next week:

_____

_____

_____

_____

_____

Declaration:

Lord, thank you for being my foundation. I trust you to keep me strong as I grow.

***

WEEK 2:
~ FAITH THAT OBEYS GOD ~

Walk faithfully. Trust completely. Obey wholeheartedly.

***

Day 8

~ Obedience Unlocks Elevation ~

📖 Scripture Focus

"And it shall come to pass, if thou shalt hearken diligently unto the voice of the Lord thy God... that the Lord thy God will set thee on high above all nations of the earth."
~ Deuteronomy 28:1 (KJV)

✍ Devotional Thought

God does not just reward faith, He rewards *obedient faith*. Obedience is what turns potential into power and promises into reality. You can believe all you want, but until belief leads to *obedience,* you're still standing at the door of elevation without walking through it.

God told Israel that if they would obey His voice and follow His commands, He would elevate them. That principle hasn't changed. Promotion in the Kingdom does not come through popularity, connections, or comfort, it comes through *submission*.

Obedience positions you for the blessing. It is not always easy. Sometimes it requires sacrifice, patience, or doing something that makes no sense to others. But elevation always follows submission.

If you want to rise, first bow in surrender. Then watch God lift you.

Reflection Thought

What is one area where God may be calling you to greater obedience? Don't delay. Write it down and make a plan to act on it today. Obedience is never wasted, it is always rewarded.

_____

_____

_____

_____

_____

_____

_____

_____

🙏 Prayer of Elevation

Lord, I want to live in a way that honors You, not just with my words, but with my obedience. Speak clearly, and I will follow. Teach me to trust You enough to do what You say, even when it is hard. I believe elevation follows obedience. In Jesus' name, Amen.

📣 Declaration For The Day

"My obedience is the key to my elevation, and I'm unlocking it today!"

Day 9

~ Love Is Proven by Obedience ~

📖 Scripture Focus
"If ye love me, keep my commandments."
~ John 14:15 (KJV)

✎ Devotional Thought

God does not measure our love by how loud we shout or how often we attend church, He measures it by how well we *listen and obey*. Jesus didn't say, "If you love Me, admire Me." He said, *"If you love Me, do what I've asked."*

Obedience isn't legalism, it is love in action. It is what separates empty religion from real relationship. When you obey God, you're saying, "I trust that You know better. I value what You say over what I feel."

Obedience isn't always convenient, but it is always powerful. Every time you obey, even when it costs you comfort or reputation, you're showing the kind of love that pleases God. And that love draws you closer, deeper, and higher in your walk with Him.

You don't have to be perfect, but you do have to be willing. Love listens. Love follows. Love obeys.

Reflection Thought

Ask yourself today: *Am I obeying God in the areas where I say I love Him most?* Write down one command or principle from God's Word that you will commit to walk out in a more intentional way this week.

_____
_____
_____
_____
_____
_____
_____
_____

Prayer of Elevation

Father, I don't want my love for You to just be words, I want it to be visible in how I live. Help me to obey You even when it is difficult. Let my love be proven through my surrender. Elevate me as I choose to honor You with obedience. In Jesus' name, Amen.

Declaration For The Day

"My love for God is more than words, it is reflected in my obedience!"

Day 10

~ Obedience in the Ordinary ~

📖 Scripture Focus
"Thus did Noah; according to all that God commanded him, so did he."
~ Genesis 6:22 (KJV)

✎ Devotional Thought

Before Noah saw a drop of rain, he swung a hammer. He didn't wait for proof, he obeyed the plan. Elevation often begins in the unseen, uncelebrated moments of obedience when no one else understands what you're doing. Noah obeyed for years, building an ark for a storm that had never happened.

That's the power of faith-fueled obedience. It is not about doing big things in big moments, it is about being faithful in the small, *ordinary* things when no one is watching.

You may not be building an ark, but you might be building a life, a ministry, a business, a family, and God is calling you to obey Him in the details: in the budget, in the boundaries, in the prayers, in the forgiveness.

Elevated faith trusts that if God gave the instruction, then the obedience is worth it, even if the outcome isn't visible yet.

Reflection Thought

Is there something you've been putting off because it does not *feel* significant or urgent? Revisit it today. Your consistency in obeying God in the little things is setting you up for the big things.

_____

_____

_____

_____

_____

_____

_____

_____

_____

Prayer of Elevation

Lord, help me obey You even when it does not make sense to others, or even to me. Teach me to build, prepare, and follow Your instructions with consistency. I trust that You see my obedience and that elevation is on the other side of it. In Jesus' name, Amen.

Declaration For The Day

"I will obey even in the ordinary, because I'm building for something greater!"

Day 11

~ Don't Just Hear It... Do It ~

📖 Scripture Focus
"But be ye doers of the word, and not hearers only, deceiving your own selves."
~ James 1:22 (KJV)

📝 Devotional Thought

Hearing the Word inspires you. *Doing* the Word transforms you. Many people sit under powerful teaching, attend services, and read devotionals, but they stop short of the most critical part……**application.**

James warns us that hearing alone can be deceptive. It can make us *feel* like we're growing when really, we're just informed but unchanged. You don't elevate by collecting sermons, you elevate by living out the Word you've heard.

The gap between hearing and doing is where many blessings are missed. Obedience is where breakthrough happens. When you put God's Word into action, when you forgive that person, give sacrificially, step out in faith, you shift from inspiration to transformation.

God is looking for *doers*. Those who will move from learning to living, from conviction to commitment. That's where elevation lives.

Reflection Thought

What's something you've heard from God recently through a sermon, devotion, or prayer that you haven't acted on yet? Make a commitment to take one step of obedience toward it today.

_____
_____
_____
_____
_____
_____
_____
_____
_____

Prayer of Elevation

God, don't let me just be a listener, I want to be a doer. I don't want to just talk about faith; I want to walk it out. Help me to apply Your Word daily so that I can grow stronger, walk wiser, and live elevated. In Jesus' name, Amen.

Declaration For The Day

"I'm not just a hearer, I'm a doer. And my obedience is elevating my life!"

Day 12

~ Obedience Is Better Than Sacrifice ~

📖 Scripture Focus
"...Behold, to obey is better than sacrifice, and to hearken than the fat of rams."
~ 1 Samuel 15:22 (KJV)

✎ Devotional Thought

God isn't impressed by performance, He's moved by obedience. Sometimes we try to trade deep surrender for shallow offerings. We give God our time, our service, even our money, but what He really wants is our *yes*.

Saul lost his kingdom not because he failed in battle, but because he failed to obey. He offered God a substitute sacrifice instead of simple submission. It is a sobering reminder that partial obedience is still disobedience, and it delays elevation.

Obedience is costly. It may cost you pride, plans, or popularity. But the reward? Unmatched favor, peace, and divine positioning. God's not asking for perfection, He's asking for your *willing heart*.

You can't out-give or outwork disobedience. Sometimes the next level isn't about *doing more*, it is about *obeying more*.

🌸 Reflection Thought:

Is there something God has asked of you that you've tried to replace with activity or "good works"? Be honest and if needed, reset your posture today. Obedience is always the better choice.

_____

_____

_____

_____

_____

_____

_____

_____

🙏 Prayer of Elevation

Lord, I don't want to offer You substitutes. I want to give You my full obedience. Help me to recognize when I'm avoiding what You asked of me. Give me the courage to obey quickly, completely, and joyfully. Elevate my life through surrendered obedience. In Jesus' name, Amen.

📣 Declaration For The Day

"I choose obedience over convenience, and God is elevating my life because of it!"

Day 13

~ Why Call Him Lord, But Don't Obey? ~

📖 Scripture Focus

"And why call ye me, Lord, Lord, and do not the things which I say?"
~ Luke 6:46 (KJV)

✎ Devotional Thought

It is easy to *call* Jesus Lord, but real power comes when you *treat* Him like Lord. The word "Lord" means Master, Ruler, and the One in charge. So, when we say, "Lord, Lord," we're acknowledging His authority, but Jesus makes it clear: saying it without *living* it is a contradiction.

Obedience is the evidence of lordship. You can sing, serve, and shout, but if you won't follow, you're missing the point. True faith submits. It does not pick and choose which instructions to obey. It follows Him fully, even when it challenges comfort zones or defies cultural trends.

Elevation does not come through empty titles, it comes through surrendered hearts. When Jesus is *truly* Lord over your life, your decisions, your relationships, and your priorities will show it.

Let today be a heart-check. Don't just give Him lip service, give Him *lordship*.

🗨 Reflection Thought

Are there any areas in your life where Jesus is Savior but not yet Lord? Identify one place where you've been resisting His authority and choose to surrender that area today.

_____
_____
_____
_____
_____
_____
_____
_____
_____

🙏 Prayer of Elevation

Jesus, I don't want to just call You Lord. I want to *live* like You're Lord. Show me the places where I've been holding back. I give You control. Rule over my heart, my thoughts, my plans, and my life. Elevate me as I yield to Your Lordship. In Your name I pray, Amen.

📣 Declaration For The Day

"Jesus is Lord over my life, and my obedience proves it!"

Day 14

~ Obedience That Leads to Glory ~

📖 Scripture Focus
"...he humbled himself, and became obedient unto death, even the death of the cross. Wherefore God also hath highly exalted him..."
~ Philippians 2:8–9 (KJV)

✎ Devotional Thought

There's no greater picture of obedience leading to elevation than Jesus. He didn't just come to earth to teach or heal, He came to *obey*. Every miracle, every word, every step toward the cross was a choice of submission. And because He humbled Himself fully, God exalted Him supremely.

This shows us a pattern: **obedience leads to elevation.** But don't miss this, Jesus' obedience wasn't easy. It cost Him everything. Yet through His surrender, *glory* followed.

If you want to be elevated by God, prepare to walk in the footsteps of Christ. That means humility over ego, surrender over strategy, and obedience over outcome. God's elevation does not always look like applause or recognition, it looks like *purpose fulfilled*.

Don't chase the spotlight. Chase obedience. God knows how to exalt those who bow low before Him.

🪧 Reflection Thought

What area of your life is requiring next-level surrendering right now? Ask yourself: *Am I willing to obey even when it costs me comfort or control?* That's where true elevation begins.

_____

_____

_____

_____

_____

_____

_____

_____

🙏 Prayer of Elevation

Jesus, thank You for modeling perfect obedience. Give me the same heart of surrender You showed on Your way to the cross. Let my life be a reflection of Your humility, and let Your glory be revealed in my walk. I trust that as I go low, You will lift me high. In Your name I pray, Amen.

 Declaration For The Day

"As I walk in obedience, God is elevating me for His glory!"

Week 2 Reflections: *Faith That Obeys God*

Reflect on how you practiced obedience this week. Think about what it looked like to trust God's instructions and walk it out in your daily life.

Where did I take a step of obedience this week?

_____

_____

_____

_____

_____

_____

How did following God's Word help me grow?

_____

_____

_____

_____

_____

_____

What is God asking me to keep obeying even when it's hard?

_____
_____
_____
_____
_____

One area I want to obey Him more fully next week:

_____
_____
_____
_____
_____

Declaration:

Lord, help me walk in full obedience to your Word and your will.

***

WEEK 3
~ FAITH THAT CONQUERS FEAR ~

Face fear. Stand brave. Keep moving forward.

***

Day 15

~ Fear Not…God Is With You ~

📖 Scripture Focus

"Fear thou not; for I am with thee: be not dismayed; for I am thy God: I will strengthen thee…"
~ Isaiah 41:10 (KJV)

✎ Devotional Thought

Fear tries to talk you out of faith. It shows up with questions, doubts, and what-ifs. But God answers fear not with explanations, but with presence. He does not always say *how* it will work, He simply says, *"I am with you."*

There's power in knowing that you're not facing life alone. The God who created the universe is walking beside you, fighting for you, and strengthening you. That alone should silence every anxious thought and every intimidating situation.

Fear shrinks your vision. Faith expands it. Fear wants to paralyze you. Faith says, "Let's go forward anyway." And the difference-maker is God's *presence*. When you know He's with you, fear loses its grip.

Don't wait for fear to disappear, move forward because God is near.

Reflection Thought

What is fear trying to block in your life right now? Name it and then declare today that it no longer has authority over your steps. You're not alone. God is with you.

_____

_____

_____

_____

_____

_____

_____

_____

Prayer of Elevation

Lord, thank You for being with me through every trial and every unknown. When fear speaks loudly, help me to hear Your voice louder. Strengthen me for the journey and remind me that with You beside me, I have nothing to fear. In Jesus' name, Amen.

 Declaration For The Day

"God is with me, I will not fear, I will rise in faith!"

Day 16

~ Fear Is Not from God ~

📖 Scripture Focus
"For God hath not given us the spirit of fear; but of power, and of love, and of a sound mind."
~ 2 Timothy 1:7 (KJV)

✎ Devotional Thought

Fear does not come from heaven. It is a lie sent to paralyze purpose. Paul reminds Timothy, and all of us, that if fear is speaking, it is not God. God gives boldness, clarity, and peace. Not panic, confusion, and dread.

If fear is trying to flood your mind, your faith must stand up and say, *"This is not from God, and it is not welcome here."* You were not created to live intimidated by life. You were built to carry power, walk in love, and make clear, courageous decisions.

Fear has a voice, but so does your faith. And today, your faith needs to speak louder. Fear says, "You can't." Faith says, "With God, I will." Fear says, "What if you fail?" Faith says, "Even if I fall, God will raise me again."

You don't need fear to survive, you need faith to thrive.

Reflection Thought

What fearful thought or "worst-case scenario" has been playing on repeat in your mind? Cancel it today. Replace it with this truth: *God gave me power. God gave me love. God gave me a sound mind.*

_____

_____

_____

_____

_____

_____

_____

_____

Prayer of Elevation

Father, thank You for reminding me that fear is not from You. I reject the spirit of fear and receive Your power, love, and sound mind. Strengthen me to walk with boldness and speak with confidence. I trust You fully. In Jesus' name, Amen.

Declaration For The Day

"Fear is not my portion…. power, love, and clarity belong to me!"

Day 17

~ When I Am Afraid, I Will Trust ~

📖 Scripture Focus
"What time I am afraid, I will trust in thee."
~ Psalm 56:3 (KJV)

📖 Devotional Thought

Faith does not deny fear, it *overcomes* it. David didn't pretend he was never afraid. He said, *"When I am afraid..."* because even the strongest warriors have moments of weakness. But what separates fear from faith is what you choose to do *next*.

You may feel the fear, but you don't have to follow it. David made a decision: *"When fear shows up, I choose to trust."* That's the shift that leads to elevation. You don't wait for the feeling of fear to disappear, you rise up and respond in trust.

Faith says, "God is bigger than this." Faith says, "I won't let this moment define me." Faith says, "I don't need to understand everything to keep moving."

Even when your knees are shaking, keep walking. Even when your heart is racing, keep believing. Trust isn't the absence of fear; it is the choice to look fear in the face and move anyway.

Reflection Thought

Is there a situation right now where fear is trying to take the lead? What would it look like to *trust* God with that instead? Choose trust on purpose today and watch how it strengthens your steps.

_____

_____

_____

_____

_____

_____

_____

_____

Prayer of Elevation

Lord, I confess that sometimes I get afraid. But today, I choose trust. When fear rises up, I will respond with faith. Teach me to lean into Your presence, stand on Your promises, and walk forward knowing You've already made a way. In Jesus' name, Amen.

Declaration For The Day

"Even when I feel fear, I choose to trust, and I will not be shaken!"

Day 18

~ Faith Walks on What Fear Drowns In ~

📖 Scripture Focus
"And he said, Come. And when Peter was come down out of the ship, he walked on the water, to go to Jesus."
~ Matthew 14:29 (KJV)

✎ Devotional Thought

Peter did what no other disciple dared to do… he *walked on water*. That wasn't just a miracle, it was the result of *faith that moved*. But notice something powerful: Peter walked *on the very thing* that should have taken him under.

That's what faith does, it allows you to walk over what fear says should drown you.

But the moment Peter shifted his focus from Jesus to the storm, fear gripped him, and he began to sink. That's still true for us today. When your eyes are on Jesus, you rise. When your eyes are on the storm, you sink.

Faith isn't about pretending the storm isn't there, it is about choosing to *step anyway,* because the One calling you is greater than what's threatening you.

If you want elevation, you have to leave the boat. The familiar. The comfortable. And say, "Lord, if it is You, I'm stepping out."

Reflection Thought

What is "the boat" for you, something comfortable but limiting? What is God calling you to step out into, even while the winds are still blowing? Bold faith does not wait for perfect conditions.

_____

_____

_____

_____

_____

_____

_____

_____

Prayer of Elevation

Jesus, give me the courage to step out of my comfort zone and into Your calling. Help me to keep my eyes on You and not on the storm. I trust You to hold me up, guide my steps, and carry me forward. I believe my elevation is on the other side of obedience. In Your name, Amen.

Declaration For The Day

"I walk by faith, not fear, what should drown me will elevate me!"

Day 19

~ Be Strong and Courageous ~

📖 Scripture Focus

"Have not I commanded thee? Be strong and of a good courage; be not afraid, neither be thou dismayed: for the Lord thy God is with thee whithersoever thou goest."
~ Joshua 1:9 (KJV)

✎ Devotional Thought

Courage isn't the absence of fear, it is the decision to move *despite* it. When God told Joshua to lead His people into the Promised Land, He didn't give him a strategy first, He gave him a *command:* "Be strong. Be courageous."

Why? Because God knew that what stood between Joshua and elevation wasn't just giants or walled cities, it was fear. Fear of failure. Fear of the unknown. Fear of leadership. But courage is the key that opens doors fear tries to lock.

You don't need a new plan, you need new boldness. God has already gone before you. Your job is to *go forward.* Every step of faith says, "God is with me, I will not be shaken."

Courage does not mean you never feel afraid. It means you trust the God who said, *"I'm going with you wherever you go."*

Reflection Thought

Where in your life do you need to stop waiting for permission and start walking in *courage?* Write it down, and today, take one intentional step forward, no matter how small.

_____

_____

_____

_____

_____

_____

_____

_____

🙏 Prayer of Elevation

Father, I receive Your command to be strong and courageous. Strengthen me for every assignment and quiet every fear that rises up. Remind me that I am never alone and that You are with me in every step. In Jesus' name, Amen.

 Declaration For The Day

"I am strong. I am courageous. I am walking boldly into my elevation!"

Day 20

~ Delivered From All My Fears ~

📖 Scripture Focus
"I sought the Lord, and he heard me, and delivered me from all my fears."
~ Psalm 34:4 (KJV)

✎ Devotional Thought

Fear does not always come in loud, obvious waves. Sometimes it creeps in silently through overthinking, hesitation, or second-guessing everything God told you. But David gives us the remedy: *"I sought the Lord."* Not social media. Not approval. Not escape. He sought **God.**

And what happened? God heard him. Not only that, *God delivered him.* Not from some fears. Not just the visible ones. But from *all* of them.

This tells us something important: you don't have to live with fear as your normal. God has the power to pull you out, to heal your mind, to settle your heart, and to restore your confidence. But first, you have to seek Him.

The more time you spend in His presence, the less power fear has over you. Because when you seek God, you find strength. You find clarity. And you find freedom.

Reflection Thought

What fear has been quietly lingering in your life? Identify it and seek the Lord in prayer today. Ask boldly for deliverance, then walk like you've already received it.

_____
_____
_____
_____
_____
_____
_____
_____

Prayer of Elevation

Lord, I'm seeking You with an open heart. You know the fears I carry, some I've spoken, and some I've hidden. But today, I give them to You. Deliver me from every fear trying to weigh me down. Elevate my faith and fill me with peace. In Jesus' name, Amen.

Declaration For The Day

"I sought the Lord, and He delivered me, fear has no hold on me!"

Day 21

~ Why Are You Afraid? Where Is Your Faith? ~

📖 Scripture Focus
"And he said unto them, Why are ye so fearful? how is it that ye have no faith?"
~ Mark 4:40 (KJV)

✍ Devotional Thought

The storm wasn't the problem. The boat wasn't the problem. The waves weren't the issue. Jesus was *right there*, and yet the disciples still panicked. That's what fear does, it blinds you to who's with you and magnifies what's against you.

Jesus didn't calm the storm first. He asked a *question* first: *"Why are you afraid?"* That's a soul-searching, elevation-stirring question. Because storms are guaranteed, but fear does not have to be.

If Jesus is in your boat, the storm can't sink you. If He said, "Let's go to the other side," then you will make it. Faith does not mean storms won't happen, it means you know who to trust in the middle of it.

Your next level requires you to anchor deeper in faith, not waver in fear. Let the storm remind you not of your weakness, but of His strength.

🌀 Reflection Thought:

What storm are you facing right now that's trying to stir fear instead of faith? Write it down, then remind yourself: *Jesus is in this with me.* Breathe, believe, and stay steady, He's still in control.

_____

_____

_____

_____

_____

_____

_____

🙏 Prayer of Elevation

Jesus, when storms rise up around me, help me to stay anchored in You. Quiet my anxious thoughts and increase my faith. Let me rest in Your presence, knowing that if You are with me, nothing can take me under. In Your name, Amen.

 Declaration For The Day

"Jesus is in my boat. I will not panic, I will trust, and I will elevate!"

Week 3 Reflection: *Faith That Conquers Fear*

Pause and look back on how you faced fear this week. Acknowledge your courage, your progress, and invite God to help you keep moving forward with bold faith.

What fears did I confront with my faith this week?

_____

_____

_____

_____

_____

How did God show me that He is bigger than my fears?

_____

_____

_____

_____

_____

Where do I still need to trust Him over my worries?

_____
_____
_____
_____
_____

One step I will take next week to keep conquering fear:

_____
_____
_____
_____
_____

Declaration:

Lord, I trust you to help me stand brave and walk by faith, not fear.

***

WEEK 4
~ FAITH TO ENDURE AND OVERCOME ~

Stay strong. Keep pressing. Victory is ahead.

***

Day 22

~ Count It All Joy ~

📖 Scripture Focus

"My brethren, count it all joy when ye fall into divers temptations; Knowing this, that the trying of your faith worketh patience."
~ James 1:2–3 (KJV)

✎ Devotional Thought

Nobody celebrates trials in the moment, but elevated faith sees *purpose* in pain. James does not say trials feel good. He says they *produce* something good. They develop patience, endurance, and spiritual maturity, things that comfort never creates.

Faith that endures does not crumble under pressure, it becomes stronger because of it. Every challenge is an opportunity to deepen your dependency on God and grow your capacity for what's next. You're not going through just to suffer, you're going through to be *strengthened*.

Joy in the midst of trials isn't denial, it is perspective. It says, "This isn't the end, it is part of the process." And because you know God is working in it, you can still praise through it.

Enduring faith looks the storm in the eye and says, *"There's joy on the other side."*

Reflection Thought

Think of one challenge you're currently facing. Instead of complaining about it, thank God for what He's producing *in you* through it. Write it down and declare joy over your process.

_____

_____

_____

_____

_____

_____

_____

Prayer of Elevation

Father, teach me to see beyond the trial. Help me count it all joy, not because of what I feel, but because of what I know You're doing in me. Strengthen my faith to endure, and let Your purpose be fulfilled through every challenge. In Jesus' name, Amen.

Declaration For The Day

"I count it all joy, this trial is building something greater in me!"

Day 23

~ Pressure Produces Perseverance ~

📖 Scripture Focus
"...but we glory in tribulations also: knowing that tribulation worketh patience; And patience, experience; and experience, hope."
~ Romans 5:3–4 (KJV)

✍ Devotional Thought

Pressure can either break you or build you. According to Paul, the pressure you're feeling isn't pointless, it is producing something powerful. Tribulation may look like a setback on the outside, but in God's economy, it is a *setup for maturity, resilience, and refined hope.*

God does not waste pain. He recycles it into perseverance. He uses the hard seasons to teach you how to stand, trust, and endure when others fold. That kind of faith can't be taught in a classroom, it is cultivated in the fire.

Your elevation is not just about being blessed, it is about being *built.* And pressure is part of the process.

So don't curse the weight, let it strengthen your spiritual muscles. You're not just going through, you're growing through.

⚪ Reflection Thought

What pressure are you under that God may be using to develop perseverance? Take a moment to write out how this season is stretching and shaping you for something greater.

_____

_____

_____

_____

_____

_____

_____

_____

_____

🙏 Prayer of Elevation

Lord, I thank You for using pressure to grow me. I may not always like it, but I trust Your purpose in it. Help me to endure, to mature, and to keep hoping. Make me stronger through what I face and prepare me for what's ahead. In Jesus' name, Amen.

 Declaration For The Day

"I'm not just under pressure, I'm under development!"

Day 24

~ Don't Grow Weary ~

📖 Scripture Focus

"And let us not be weary in well doing: for in due season, we shall reap, if we faint not."
~ Galatians 6:9 (KJV)

✎ Devotional Thought

Doing the right thing can get exhausting, especially when the results don't come quickly. You pray, serve, give, forgive, and sometimes it feels like nothing is changing. But the Word reminds us: *don't give up.* Why? Because there's a *due season* with your name on it.

Enduring faith understands that delay is not denial. Every seed you've sown in faith is being watered, even if you can't see the growth yet. The enemy wants you to faint right before the harvest, but God says, *"Keep going."*

Elevation does not come to the most talented or the most visible, it comes to the *faithful.* If you stay planted, stay consistent, and stay obedient, your due season will find you.

Don't quit on the promise because the process is long. You're closer than you think.

Reflection Thought

Where have you been tempted to give up lately? Take a moment to write down what you're believing God for. Then speak this over it: *"I will not faint, I will reap in due season."*

_____
_____
_____
_____
_____
_____
_____
_____

Prayer of Elevation

Lord, thank You for reminding me that You see my faithfulness, even when others don't. Strengthen me when I feel tired. Keep my heart encouraged and my hands steady. I believe my season is coming, and I will not give up. In Jesus' name, Amen.

Declaration For The Day

"I will not faint. I'm sowing in faith and reaping in due season!"

Day 25

~ Wait On the Lord ~

📖 Scripture Focus
"But they that wait upon the Lord shall renew their strength; they shall mount up with wings as eagles..."
~ Isaiah 40:31 (KJV)

✎ Devotional Thought

Waiting isn't wasted time, it is preparation time. When God says "wait," He's not putting your life on hold, He's preparing your strength for the next level. Elevated faith learns how to trust God in the waiting room.

We live in a world that hates to wait. But the Kingdom of God grows in seasons. The eagle does not rush, it rises at the right wind. And so will you.

While you're waiting, God is renewing. While you're still, He's strengthening. He's teaching you to soar not in your own power, but in *His*.

Waiting does not mean doing nothing, it means doing the right things with the right heart. Keep praying. Keep serving. Keep believing. Because when the time is right, elevation won't be a climb, it'll be a *lift*.

Reflection Thought

Are you in a waiting season? Ask yourself: what is God strengthening in me right now? Write down what you're learning in the wait and thank Him for the growth that's happening even in silence.

_____
_____
_____
_____
_____
_____
_____
_____

Prayer of Elevation

Lord, thank You for the strength that comes in the wait. Teach me to trust Your timing and rest in Your process. Help me to see this season not as a delay, but as divine development. I believe You are renewing me for greater. In Jesus' name, Amen.

Declaration For The Day

"I'm not just waiting, I'm being renewed for my elevation!"

Day 26

~ Pressed But Not Crushed ~

📖 Scripture Focus

"We are troubled on every side, yet not distressed; we are perplexed, but not in despair; Persecuted, but not forsaken; cast down, but not destroyed."
~ 2 Corinthians 4:8–9 (KJV)

✍ Devotional Thought

Life will press you, but it does not have the power to *crush* you. Paul reminds us that trials may surround us, but they don't have to *sink* us. Elevated faith knows how to be under pressure without falling apart.

You may be hit, but you're not helpless. You may feel stretched, but you're not shattered. Why? Because your strength does not come from the outside, it comes from the God who lives *within*.

The enemy wants you to believe the pressure means defeat. But the truth is, pressure is often proof that purpose is pushing through. It is in the crushing that the oil flows. It is in the breaking that the blessing is released.

You're still here for a reason. If life hasn't taken you out, then God's not done yet.

Reflection Thought

What's been pressing you lately? Instead of focusing on the weight, declare the Word over it. Say: *"I may be pressed, but I will not be crushed. God is holding me together."*

_____

_____

_____

_____

_____

_____

_____

_____

Prayer of Elevation

Lord, thank You that no matter how much life presses me, I am not defeated. Remind me daily that Your power sustains me when I feel weak. Let every trial I face bring forth strength, oil, and glory. In Jesus' name, Amen.

Declaration For The Day

"I'm pressed but not crushed. God is keeping me and lifting me higher!"

Day 27

~ Your Faith Is More Precious Than Gold ~

📖 Scripture Focus

"That the trial of your faith, being much more precious than of gold that perisheth... might be found unto praise and honour and glory at the appearing of Jesus Christ."
~ 1 Peter 1:7 (KJV)

✎ Devotional Thought

Gold is refined in fire, but your faith is even more valuable than gold. That means the trials you face aren't just random hardships, they're part of a holy refining. God is not punishing you, He's *proving* you.

Every trial has a purpose: to purify your trust, strengthen your endurance, and bring glory to God through your life. Fire does not destroy real faith, it reveals it. What you're going through isn't just testing your limits, it is producing a legacy.

Faith that's never tested can't be trusted. But faith that endures the fire comes out unshakable, undeniable, and unstoppable.

Your trial is temporary, but the glory God will reveal through it is eternal. Hold on. He's doing more in you than you can imagine.

Reflection Thought

How has your faith been tested recently? Take a moment today to reflect not just on the challenge, but on the growth. Write down one way this season has made your faith stronger.

_____

_____

_____

_____

_____

_____

_____

_____

_____

Prayer of Elevation

Lord, thank You for refining my faith through the fire. Even when I don't understand the process, I trust Your purpose. Make my faith pure, strong, and unshakable. Let it bring You glory in every season. In Jesus' name, Amen.

Declaration For The Day

"My faith is worth more than gold, it is being refined for greater!"

Day 28

~ Hold Fast to Your Confession ~

📖 Scripture Focus
"Let us hold fast the profession of our faith without wavering; (for he is faithful that promised;)"
~ Hebrews 10:23 (KJV)

✍ Devotional Thought

When life shakes you, what comes out of your mouth? In seasons of pressure, what you *say* matters. Hebrews reminds us to hold tightly to our confession, what we believe, what we declare, and what we know to be true about God.

Faith does not just live in your heart, it lives on your lips. Elevation requires consistency, even when conditions change. When your emotions waver, your confession shouldn't.

Speak faith until it becomes your default. Speak hope until your heart aligns. Speak truth until your thoughts surrender. Why? Because *He is faithful that promised.*

Your confession won't always match your circumstances, but it will align you with God's character. And He's never failed.

So hold fast. Keep speaking. Keep standing. Your words of faith are paving the road to your elevation.

🎤 Reflection Thought:

What have you been speaking lately, faith or frustration? Take a moment to write out a new confession rooted in God's promises. Speak it aloud today and hold fast to it.

_____

_____

_____

_____

_____

_____

_____

_____

🙏 Prayer of Elevation

God, help me to hold fast to what You've promised, even when life tries to shake me. Let my words reflect my trust in You. Strengthen me to speak life, truth, and victory especially when it is hard. I believe You are faithful, and I stand on Your Word. In Jesus' name, Amen.

📣 Declaration For The Day

"I hold fast to my faith. God is faithful, and I'm rising with bold confession!"

Week 4 Reflection: *Faith to Endure and Overcome*

Look back on this week and recognize how you pressed on when things got tough. Give God thanks for giving you strength to endure and courage to keep overcoming.

How did I see God help me endure through challenges this week?

_____
_____
_____
_____
_____
_____

What did I overcome that I couldn't do in my own strength?

_____
_____
_____
_____
_____
_____

Where do I need to keep standing strong and not give up?

_____
_____
_____
_____
_____

One truth I will hold on to next week to help me overcome:

_____
_____
_____
_____
_____

Declaration:

Lord, thank you for giving me strength to endure. I will keep pressing forward with faith.

***

WEEK 5

~ FAITH TO ELEVATE OTHERS ~

Lift others. Serve well. Inspire growth.

***

Day 29

~ Let Your Light Shine ~

📖 Scripture Focus

"Let your light so shine before men, that they may see your good works, and glorify your Father which is in heaven."
~ Matthew 5:16 (KJV)

✎ Devotional Thought

Faith was never meant to be hidden. Elevated faith does not just lift you, it lights the way for others. Jesus calls us the light of the world, not just to shine in church buildings, but in boardrooms, classrooms, neighborhoods, and everyday conversations.

Your light is your witness. It is how you handle pressure. It is how you treat people. It is how you respond when others are watching and especially when they aren't.

People may never read the Bible, but they're reading *you*. Let them see a faith that's real, consistent, and contagious. You don't have to be perfect, you just have to be *visible*. Because your light points them to Him.

Shining does not mean being flashy, it means being faithful. And when you live lit by faith, God gets the glory.

Reflection Thought

How are you letting your light shine right now? Who in your life may need to see your faith in action? Ask God to show you how to be a light to someone today through love, kindness, or truth.

_____
_____
_____
_____
_____
_____
_____
_____

Prayer of Elevation

Lord, I don't want to hide the faith You've placed in me. Help me to shine with purpose and love. Let my life reflect You clearly so others are drawn to Your light. Use me today to encourage, influence, and inspire. In Jesus' name, Amen.

Declaration For The Day

"I am a light in the darkness, my faith points others to God!"

Day 30

~ Run Your Race With Bold Faith ~

📖 Scripture Focus
"Let us run with patience the race that is set before us, Looking unto Jesus the author and finisher of our faith..."
~ Hebrews 12:1–2 (KJV)

✍ Devotional Thought

You've made it to Day 30 not just of this devotional, but of a deeper journey of faith. And the message today is simple: *Don't stop here.* The race isn't over. Elevation is not a moment, it is a lifestyle. And God has more ahead.

The scripture reminds us that this is *your* race. Not theirs. Not someone else's path. Yours. With your story, your timing, and your pace. Run it with endurance. Walk it with trust. Live it with bold faith.

But don't run aimlessly, *look to Jesus.* He started this faith in you, and He's committed to finishing it. He's already ahead of you, cheering you on, guiding every step. When it gets hard, when it feels slow, when the path is unclear, *keep your eyes on Him.*

You're not just called to start in faith. You're called to finish strong. And elevation awaits every step you take in trust.

🌿 Reflection Thought

As you close this 30-day journey, what has God stirred in you? What step of bold faith is He calling you to take next? Write it down, commit it to prayer, and then *run your race.*

_____

_____

_____

_____

_____

_____

_____

_____

🙏 Final Prayer of Elevation

Lord, thank You for bringing me through this journey of faith. Let everything I've learned take root in my spirit. Help me to live daily in bold, elevated faith. I fix my eyes on You the Author, the Finisher, the One who holds my future. I will run. I will trust. I will rise. In Jesus' name, Amen.

📣 Final Declaration For The Day

"This is just the beginning, I'm running with bold faith, and I'm built to finish strong!"

Closing Thought: *Don't Stop Here*

You've done more than read a devotional, you've walked through a spiritual shift.

For 30 days, you've built, stretched, tested, and elevated your faith. But this isn't the finish line, this is the *foundation*.

Now take what you've journeyed through over the last 30 days and let it become your daily rhythm. Let these truths take root in your routine, in your thoughts, and in your bold decisions.

The enemy would love nothing more than for this fire to flicker out after Day 30. But God is calling you to take what you've learned and live it out loud:

- Let your prayers carry more confidence.
- Let your words reflect what you believe.
- Let your faith set the atmosphere everywhere you go.

You may not feel different but keep walking. You may still face battles but keep trusting. You've been equipped to not just survive the seasons ahead, but to *conquer* them in faith.

Don't wait for a new mountain to build new momentum. The journey has already begun. And your elevation continues from here.

Now That You've Finish: *My Faith to Elevate Reflection*

Congratulations on completing your 30-day Faith to Elevate journey! Take this moment to pause, look back, and look ahead. Use these questions to capture what God has shown you and to stay focused on moving forward with purpose.

1. What have I gained from this journey?
(What truths, lessons, or moments have strengthened my faith?)

_____
_____
_____
_____
_____
_____
_____
_____
_____
_____
_____
_____
_____
_____
_____

2. What are my faith goals moving forward?
(What new habits, prayers, or actions will help me continue to grow?)

3. How will I keep elevating?
(Who can I share this with? How can I stay accountable? What next steps will help me keep rising in faith, family, and purpose?)

_____
_____
_____
_____
_____
_____
_____
_____
_____
_____
_____
_____
_____

Declaration:
By faith, I will keep rising. I will keep believing. I will keep elevating.

Scripture Reference Index

Acts

- Acts 3:6–8 – Day 25

Deuteronomy

- Deuteronomy 28:1–2 – Day 8

Ephesians

- Ephesians 3:20 – Day 29

Galatians

- Galatians 6:2 – Day 24
- Galatians 6:9 – Day 23
- Galatians 3:11 – (Referenced thematically)

Genesis

- Genesis 6:22 – Day 10

Habakkuk

- Habakkuk 2:4 – Day 4

Hebrews

- Hebrews 11:1 – Day 1
- Hebrews 10:23 – Day 28
- Hebrews 12:1–2 – Day 30

Isaiah

- Isaiah 40:31 – Day 25
- Isaiah 41:10 – Day 15

James

- James 1:2–4 – Day 22
- James 1:22 – Day 11
- James 2:17 – Day 6

John

- John 14:15 – Day 9

Joshua

- Joshua 1:9 – Day 19

Luke

- Luke 6:46 – Day 13

Mark

- Mark 4:39–40 – Day 21
- Mark 11:22–24 – Day 3

Matthew

- Matthew 5:16 – Day 29
- Matthew 14:29–31 – Day 18
- Matthew 25:40 – Day 27

Philippians

- Philippians 2:4 – Day 26
- Philippians 2:8–9 – Day 14

Proverbs

- Proverbs 3:5–6 – Day 7

Psalm

- Psalm 34:4 – Day 20
- Psalm 56:3 – Day 17

Romans

- Romans 1:17 – (Referenced thematically)
- Romans 5:3–5 – Day 23
- Romans 10:17 – Day 2
- Romans 1:12 – Day 30

2 Corinthians

- 2 Corinthians 4:8–9 – Day 26
- 2 Corinthians 5:7 – Day 5

2 Peter

- 1 Peter 1:6–7 – Day 27

2 Timothy

- 2 Timothy 1:7 – Day 16

1 Samuel

- 1 Samuel 15:22 – Day 12

1 Thessalonians

- 1 Thessalonians 5:11 – Day 24

Acknowledgments

To my wife, **Umeka Wright**
My partner in life, love, and ministry.

Thank you for walking with me through every season. For praying with me, believing in me, and loving me beyond titles or tasks. Your strength behind the scenes, your grace in public, and your unwavering faith have lifted me more than words can express.

You challenge me to grow, cover me in prayer, and remind me what love that reflects Christ really looks like. This devotional would not be what it is without your presence, your encouragement, and your belief in the calling God placed on my life.

I honor you. I appreciate you. I love you.
Always.

~ **Hubby**

A Final Word of Thanks

To every reader who has journeyed through these 30 days, **Thank you.**

Thank you for opening your heart to this devotional.
Thank you for trusting God's voice, even when the way wasn't clear.
Thank you for showing up with faith, even when fear tried to hold you back.

My prayer is that *Faith to Elevate!* has not only stirred your spirit, but also shifted your walk. That you have discovered new strength, deeper clarity, and renewed confidence in the God who calls you *higher*.

This isn't the end, it is the launchpad. Keep believing. Keep building. Keep climbing.

And remember:
You were never meant to stay where you started. You were created to elevate.

With gratitude and expectation,
Dr. Slavoski L. Wright Sr.

www.ingramcontent.com/pod-product-compliance
Lightning Source LLC
Chambersburg PA
CBHW031636160426
43196CB00006B/441